The Reach is (W)holy~

poetry inspired by the sacred

by

Wendy Candida Havlir Cherry

Building altars out of words. . .

This book is dedicated to the process of revealing what is whole, holy, and healing. Without my sacred teachers, and they are many, these little heart sanctuaries would not be possible. These "altars" are tiny offerings to each and every one of them. I also want to thank my mother for the gifts of clear seeing, creativity, and great strength. And, to my father, I am grateful for untamed victory and wild reclamation. Finally, this is for Randall, my original inspiration. You are in every poem.

Emergence

There was nothing
and then
there was you,

combing my hair.

Wings

Set down the weight,
you are only here for a moment.

Let yourself belong to whatever you love.

Blessing Bowl

Move softly in,
caress your strength,
it doesn't have to be hard~

write a new story
rest inside that place
where grace and fierceness
reside.

Cultivating Yin

In the long velvet of the night
creeping in and out of undone dreams
I cup my hands
catching each struggle
in the (w)holiness of my palms.

Shell and Yolk

This morning, I love
the longing
the ache
the having
the holding
the dirt on the window
the spider by the bowl
the magic altar
the big let go.

.

Grace

Child spirit takes my hand,
she is wild sweetness
giggling, with
grass stained knees and dandelion hair
leading me back
to diamond clear eyes,
big love heart,
and the trusted whisper of
yes.

Gathering Place

Are you willing to choose
what you belong to~
stand in your truth,
bearing scars carved deep
into your sacred skin?

Are you willing to let
the hot rolling air of your own acceptance
cover your flesh,
smoothing the wrinkled pages
of your old, discarded stories?

Can you meet your breath where it wants to be seen~
where it longs for you
to notice
the way it chooses you
over and over again
with full-blown, absolute devotion?

You. Yes, you~
beautiful lineage holder,
how will you stand in your truth?
Sing over your bones and
those who breathed before you?

Are you willing to get messy,
to look foolish and be scared,
to rearrange your beliefs, move toward yourself
like a brand new lover,
with the song and blessing of all your desire?

Will you allow yourself to fit more fully
into your belonging

and the exquisite curves of your (w)holiness?

Will you look
when I strike the match
revealing my unearthed and golden cracks
leading back to the sparkling spiral of my heart?

Can you see the light that nourishes you
and me
and all of us
because it comes from the one true luminosity?

Are you willing to love what you love,
abandon all else and
be the poet of your own heart?

I can tell you
that somewhere beneath the hiding sliding surface of illusion
is a numinous gathering place
where all your parts are wanted, welcome, and wildly
adored.

Go find that place.

Reclaiming the Ring

It was simple
I woke-up
when I realized~

I choose myself.

Clear Seeing

A poem was writing me last night
small inscriptions on my dreaming eyelids
asking me to move forward
into the center
of my heart's promise.

Home

I have arrived, here, inside these bones~
admiring the sparkle and dust.

Choose

She noticed her heart was feeling tight and scared
and decided to trust the doorway of her own
wise council.

Radical Embodiment

When others seemingly reject you
you are still (w)holy.

When you reject yourself
you are still (w)holy.

When you feel anything at all
you are still (w)holy.

Drop the dress,
reveal your skin~
you are the perfect altar.

Coming Back

Light the lantern of your heart,
let it show you the way.

Sacred Unfolding

I will choose to walk in trust
while also holding sadness.
Arigato zaishö~
I bring blessings to the obstacles.

Be

The Hopi Elders say the river is moving very fast
that we should let go, let the swift stream carry us.

This unknown,
feet can't touch bottom,
don't know what will happen next,
where the river will take me kind of being~
is an undoing,
an untying of the well-known knots worn thin from tight
grasping,
tumbling into the vast unseen.

Turn toward what you belong to.
Turn toward the fear, the hope, the shock, the sorrow,
turn toward the unknown,
trusting the view will be provided.

And turn toward the known beauty~
hold it in the palms of your hands.

Float

As the river moves me
I remember
to trust myself.

Synchronicity

Black crow on the right
stars bearing witness above
and you
stepping out before me~

big medicine
gentle love.

Protection

Sweet child spirit
I see you.

I witness you
whispering your fears into the sacred container
offered from one who knows.

May you feel
deep in your little, growing bones
just how sacred and loved you are.

Pilgrimage

Your eyes fall on me,
I ask for grace

I only know
this
is
what
saves
me.

Laughter

He knocked at the door with his giant, god-like paw~
I invited him in and wrestled him
to the floor.

Frontier

Stunned, I follow him up the stairs~
we climb out of my head. "See," he says,

"it's here, it's here."

See-Saw

He is God
pretending to be my lover,
leading me home.

Barbie Gone Bad

She looks in the mirror~
who in the hell are you?
I am perfection, don't you recognize me?

Chalice

Her power source is different now.

No more plugging in
or extension cords,
or looking to the crowd.

Her power rests
inside her flesh,
trusting the roundness of her body,
supple softness rising up,
from all her healing stories.

Your Hallelujah

Sometimes
it can be
as simple
as locating
what's working~

sometimes, it's all we have.

I don't have many answers,
only a Herculean
wanting
longing
to bring some ease

for you
for me

for the mom who believes
she isn't good enough,
for the child afraid of the dark,
the water that won't stop rising,
the roses blowing apart,

and the despair
when everything
seems lost.

Today I offer a simple, quiet space for the flooding of her tears,
tell her I'm not going anywhere~

She is my hallelujah.

Sacred Gesture

What could today feel like
if we softened into the longing
that burns inside?
wildfire longing~
the kind betrayed for hate and fear,
grief and despair.

I wonder if you can remember
where to gather the nectar
that will keep you moving forward,
toward you,
toward us,
and all the goodness in the world?

So many have forgotten.

So many are in pain
at a loss
on their knees,
asking how to proceed.

I know despair,
the hopelessness that freezes
the warmest heart.

I beg you,
find your hallelujah~

we need more, so many more, hallelujahs.

Wild Woman Within

You were there in my dream
standing in beautiful
I belong with you,

I keep sending love poems in the dark.

Heart Door

When you knock
and there's no answer,
it's not your door~

leave a blessing anyway.

Expecting Miracles

Wild unknown
I bow to you

leaning in
with curiosity

into the scary places
only I can go

dressed in something strange
and new.

Wild Yes

He said I could be a lion tamer~

I
am
the
lion
tamed
and
the wild roar,
these lips know the kiss of both.

Great Dark Wing

There is shadow
in everything

I want to dress myself in its skin, too~
to understand the pain
lodged in the velvety remedy beneath.

This I can choose
because there is no choice
if I want to be free
and in love
with anything at all.

Feather and Bone

Do not let your winged spirit be caged~

trust
your
wild.

Initiation

When the river rises
get out of your own way
let it come, dear one

tears are remedy for a parched soul,
and mark the (w)holiest of days.

Come for Tea

This being a guesthouse
is the highest honor

walking in both worlds
through the sacred, hidden door

where everything is medicine~
our bones are nothing but love
and star fire.

Wind and Water

There is no difference between
wild and holy~
you are both.

Chispa

There's too much to lose
when you don't trust your fire.
Let it light the way,
into your wilderness.

Illumination

There are things
I would not know
had I not decided to sing
over the aching
inside my bones.

Precipice

The strength of her legs
standing firm
inside the question,

and another door swings open.

The Truth About Softness

My body is my blessing~
she holds
my heart.

Hearth Space

Hidden inside her skin
a wildfire was blazing
it came and went
quick enough, but
every time she knew
the great rewiring was taking place~

new wisdom rising
on wings of unstoppable knowing.

Maestra

I've seen her
slipping between the worlds
an almost invisible alchemy.

Today she arrived
inside the pink sparkle heart
of a wiggly child
who giggled, and said,
the teacher resides in each of us~
we all have medicine to share.

Hope

Listen,
your heart
has poetry for you.

Made in the USA
San Bernardino, CA
26 April 2018